Sleet at Dusk

A George Washington Story

Sleet at Dusk

A George Washington Story

Poems by

Edward McCrorie

Cover design by Shay Culligan
Cover image by Benjamin de Young, "Brown Tree Branch in
Daytime" at Unsplash.com

ISBN: 978-1-63980-032-2

Kelsay Books
502 South 1040 East, A-119
American Fork, Utah 84003
Kelsaybooks.com

Dedicated to Beatrice,
on a par with Penelopeia

Introduction

Though the story, obviously, is not new of George Washington crossing the Delaware—how often it's been pictured and painted!—I felt it needed to be told again now to Americans, both to stress the wintertime facts, heaven itself seeming to shout NO! to the river's crossing, and to underscore the severely stressed mind and muscle of the General.

My task was enormous in every way. So I called on sources I had come to love and admire long ago. I had turned out well received translations of Virgil and Homer, each of the three epics focusing on a single man's struggle to see his way home, to fight off inner and outer antagonists, to unite with sometimes dubious powers above and below, and to achieve a final, admirable peace.

Curiously, Virgil's *Aeneid* followed the style of Homer's *Iliad* and *Odyssey*. All three epics use a meter called dactylic hexameter: the music that resulted moves the story along fairly fast, but the line is usually called a "falling" one, because it ends, to borrow the jazz expression of "downbeat" in the blues, on a somber note. It's also worth remembering that the Greek word for epic poet is *aeidos*, meaning "singer." Homer also accompanied himself with a stringed instrument.

So my readers now may feel the mild or serious threat of a downfall as each line ends. But that threat did not stop Aeneas from winning his final battle at Rome, nor did it stop Odysseus, for all his woes, from reuniting with Penelope at Ithaca, their home. Nor did such a threat stop Washington—who often was slowed down—from achieving victory at Trenton, and eventually a final victory over Cornwallis at Yorktown. America still belongs to Americans, not to those Brits.

Edward McCrorie

Contents

Part 1: No Help from the Heavens   11

Part 2: The Camp David   14

Part 3: Battle Cry   21

Part 1: No Help from the Heavens

Hang-down willow trees by the Delaware River.
Half-formed bodies of ice midstream in December,
sycamores' bared muscle—the god-playing north-wind
laughing them down. This harsh Christmas the Hessian
soldiers housed at Trenton, warmed by their east coast
plunder and dark rum, toasted the Christ-child,
Germany and triumph. They carved mutton and pig-meat,
drowsed at dusk, and American hearth-fires guttered.

Many pictured Washington likely a doomed name,
Brits in command of Philadelphia shortly,
Congress burned and Jefferson hanged, the ash-rise
black bits of *li-ber-ty* flecking a drab cloud,
white and black men both vassals of King George.

General George Washington stared at the dun sky's
ranks of untiring wind and sleet as they harrowed
every coccyx, leveled saplings and lowered
shabby pennons—New York, New Jersey, Virginia.
How to advance where snow maundered like empty
swarms of advice? Where John Hancock had longed for
'just one victory soon' in yesterday's mail-sack?
'All our cause in Congress thins like a late moon.'

Men along the river, stumps in a dead swamp,
blurred in the whelming storm that swirled like a great king's
empire churning tribes and nations like butter.
Doom the storm kept droning, or *Farce!* with a thousand
jokes in the army's eyes. The General stood still,
tall and hard as the blue spruce-tree behind him.
Yet his heart quailed for the loss of his men's faith,
spirits fading again like loosening, fear-struck
bowels. Though a fool whispered inside him
Cross that river, a sage counseled him *Don't fight.*

'Don't be a fool, Commander. Leave in the morning,
mend your farm-boy troops by the calm Susquehanna.'
General Horatio Gates, reared as a gentle
Briton, now not gentle with Brits, had warned him,
'Battle with Hessians? Feed your army to black bears!'
Washington listened well: Gates had the eighteenth
century squared on his shoulders: clarity, reason,
war like a loom, the weft and warping of young men
trained in the ordered age of Newton and numbers.
Heaven and earth made rounds of harmony dancing,
drum and fifer afield, above them the fixed stars.
Ah, but Washington hurling battalions at pre-dawn
madness at Trenton? Gates thought not. A nor'easter,
not some cosmic plan, but chaos and panic
ruled the air. Why not red Susquehanna
hearths all winter then, and plans for a *spring* fight?

Even black oaks now were letting the last leaves
go in the gale's talons. Pine-stands upriver
felt their wrists somehow broken, and old woods,
miles of Pennsylvania mountains, were disarmed.
Had the General's ragged militia beheld them
they'd have wailed, 'All America's falling!'
So after the man told him, 'Run from this battle,'
Gates marched south, complaining of illness.

Washington's brain, like a horse's, was piebald,
black and white, but stalled. The Delaware sided
coolly with Gates, with a moaned *No* from New Jersey's
wind-blown underbrush. Just last week the Commander,
writing his brother, conceded: 'At Trenton we can't win.'
Still he told commanders, the restive, the anxious,
'Rouse your men for a long night's march with a two-days'
pouch of cooked food.' Soldiers were marshaled,

pricked by rumors. Washington thought if the men knew
Trenton's the target, German bayonets waiting,
hundreds would fly to the woods like starlings in thunder.
No one must know then, no one could possibly feel out
stars to predict thin hope—in Washington's lifeline?
Hessians vanquished, Brits routed on all fronts?
Howe and Cornwallis gone cannonsmoke, wrong flags?

No. The General moped. Martha's engaging
hand was far as the delft, springtime Potomac.
All her George could do on a loveless December
night was look to some men nearby. The iron
foundry man, Nathanael Greene, would proudly
name his first two children George and Martha.
Henry Knox from Boston, huge in his fight-plans,
huge in his walk—they called him the Artillery War-god.
Yes, and William Lee, the General's best close
man, a slave: when his master died he would go free.
But walking toward him now, eighteen and already
New York Gunnery Captain, Alexander Hamilton
asked him, 'Soon, sir, are we crossing to Jersey?'
'Cannons go later,' Washington answered,
doubting anyone's crossing. 'Tell me the storm will
end, Alex.' 'I'd never fathom a god this
wild, General.' Pause. Then trying to change things,
'Maybe a moment, sir, for warmth in the tavern?
Milk and rum, good news and a young friend?'

Washington sighed, then walked uphill to the tavern
past colonials trying to mantle their powder,
hectic brigade commanders and Gloucester boatmen,
cannoneers with chitin-like knuckles at hard work.

Part 2: The Camp David

Suddenly women indoors heating the dark rum,
lavender bonnets, brows beaded with milk-steam,
honed cheeses, honey, cinnamon, hot buns.
Just-grilled buckwheat flapjacks piled on a corner
table were eyed then stormed and leveled by young men.
Washington liked one green-eyed woman to serve him,
Beth she was called, the same name as his Betsy—
no, not his—this Beth was gentle and somber,
not like the girl he'd asked to marry him. Fifteen,
airy as whey, *No,* she'd said. And again *No.*
How his heart and fingers had palsied composing
London-like verse to his love! Each word was a dead bird
now. Betsy was forty, a mother. For six years
after her No, Washington courted no woman.

Sam McKonkey welcomed Washington loudly,
though he'd tired as host. He cooked for the soldiers,
spelled out whims of the Delaware, damned the British
crown and claimed, 'Only the General outranks me!'
Hamilton smiled, saluted McKonkey and toasted
milk-warmed rum with Washington. 'General Ewing
sends good news—he'll help, sir, whatever the winter.'
Hamilton gave him the sodden message. He could not
know what hurt the Commander, later dispatches
curled in the man's bag like nestlings without wings:
'Weather is worse and worse, General.' 'Can't cross.'
Ewing could only lob some shot—if the battle
joined at all—from the far side of the river.

Change had come for Washington, listening always,
often from plain Americans close by. And slowly—
losing Betsy, he'd found Martha—in ten years.
Finding Martha, he'd not fathered a child yet,
though she'd carried two before she was widowed.

Well then. Decide to cross! he thought. But he might not,
what with December careening, elderly beech-trees'
blood drying, phloem stalled in the iced rain.
While each thicket and grove, beaver and woodchuck
might have succumbed to wintry underworld nightmares,
Washington turned again to listen when two young
troops approached at Hamilton's call and saluted.
One was known to him; the other, a boy, was a stranger.
'Here's a friend, sir,' Hamilton said of the younger.
'Martin rejoined the Rhode Island regiment last week.
Soldiers call him our "Camp David." He sings well,
raising spirits not with a lyre but a jew's harp.'
'Bible heights,' Washington asked, 'for a camp-song?'
'Martin hails from Providence, famous for Roger
Williams' faith,' said Hamilton. 'One of my Williams
grandfathers, General,' Martin told him, 'bravely
married a Narragansett woman. I'm red too.'
Washington mused. 'You're both savage and saint then?'
'Both my Williams and tribal people have told me
peace comes first, General, loving the strangers
living amongst us.' 'Why then join a militia
fighting ice and foreigners, Brits and their hirelings?'
'Hoping to change minds, sir. War can be drastic
song but true. And to tame Goliath, my new friend.'

Washington nodded toward the face of the second
private staring hard, the eyes like a tomcat's
paws tight on his cheeks. 'Goliath,' the latest
name for this well-paid spy reporting to two men,
General Greene and himself, had uniformed oddly,
sporting a blue-etched powder horn and a silk scarf.
Washington said, 'No Bible giant but well dressed.
Are you also a singer? Or merely a soldier?'
'I don't play, sir,' Goliath answered. 'And I'm no

mammoth hero. I shrank because of the scanty
vice in American camps. I used to be massive
thirst and gluttony, greed, drunkenness, mad ruts.
Now no sin is in sight. Like Catholics, the army
cramps from imposed fasts. Even the camp dogs
prey like monks and nuns.' The plight of Goliath
won him frowns and chuckles. 'Anger and pride, though,'
David said, 'are my man's merits. I call him
Ears too, Commander, for I am the peaceful
voice inside him.' Hamilton broke in smiling,
'Now we should hear you sing.' The tavern became still.

David plucked his harp, waited, and started:
'Walk the Blackstone River in autumn
where warblers lack the gold of the past spring,
lack desire, prowess, a vision of nesting,
and stay no longer. Wings renewed for the long flight
south to a cheerless winter, I barely remember
you in May, warbling notes about silence.'

Though he liked the song, a barbed nostalgia
stuck in Washington's side. He applauded but shut down
fancies of home and called out, 'Warrior David,
Bible king! You know he spotted Bathsheba
bathing at dusk, naked. How can a body
make a man murder? He ordered her husband
first into battle, Uriah was killed, and Bathsheba
came to her king. So you, if you see a delightful
farm-girl tonight, will your drop your arms and desert us?'
Martin answered, 'Sir, my lover is far off.'
Washington threw his rum at the hearth and commanded,
'Sing us a war-song then. A victory bonfire!

You're a soldier, aren't you? Fifers and snare drums.'
David answered, 'Yes, sir.' He pondered, awaiting
mood and moment. As though he'd pocketed giant
killing stones, his voice spiraled, a great sling—

'Joseph Warren! Boston doctor, you tended
dozens of soldiers' wounds, hip-joint and elbow
pocked by grapeshot. You answered each dying
moan with a hummed lullaby. Healer and tearful
good-bye man, you listened and rushed to the loudest
screams at Bunker Hill where blood from a teen-aged
private jetted, your face close to his red nape,
seconds to live. While muskets crackled at climbing
British again, the hillside covered with jerking,
bleeding redcoats—rage and folly on both sides—
one boy's lungs were both suddenly blown out,
struck by a marksman, a single shot at the one chest.
Prophet as well as doctor and soldier, you knew well:
all our weapons, soon emptied of lead tongues,
Cambridge militiamen ran off, bayonets chased them,
Brits at their backs, buttocks and hamstrings.
Where you bandaged your last man's
forehead a shrike-like enemy saw you
and stooped fast, drove your face into
dirt and—oh, I can feel it hard at

my head, the break-through
ball from that pistol's all-out
pain, my mind is in lightning.'

David paused. Then sang, striking the one string:
'Our side won: we lost ground but we killed men.
Their side won: they lost men but they gained land.
Doctor Warren, who can temper your short life
after you salved so many soldiers' future?
Boston mourned you, praised the rest who had fallen,
missed at dusk. Plainsong, burial, drum roll.
No one sang for the wounded. Those you wept for
lacking hands, an eye, or lost in their own heads
after the king's crazed rifle-butts brained them.
Femur crushed, a major abruptly grey-haired,
never to walk despite the splints of your hard love.
Where were the bells, a scant newspaper column
minding their pain? Must war history reckon
only dead buildings, tombstones, a new debt?
No man injured, beggared, plopped on a back street?'

'I was lucky, Commander, left with a slight limp
thanks to Doctor Warren, killed in the battle.
Still I feel his warm hand on my slow leg.'

Beth and some close friends wept. Though he had shed no
tears, Washington touched the harp in David's
hand and said, 'Come back, good voice, with another
song soon. And you, named Ears? Goliath?
Watch and care for my harper.'
Ears had listened, his face plain as a panther's.
Martin Williams said, 'Nik-WEN-um, Commander—
I am going home now. Roger Williams
wrote down words of Narragansetts he sat with.'
Martin left for the low tent of Goliath—
not for his Providence love—'AH-weh-tah-WAH-twok,

19

Narragansett, sir, for "We are a good match.'"
Hamilton told him afterwards, 'Martin was down, sir,
seven days in a Boston hospital.' 'Go find
General Greene or Colonel Varnum and tell him,'
Washington ordered, 'march those two in the rear guard.'

Part 3: Battle Cry

General John Sullivan, Washington's best young
leader under pressure, finding his Irish
wrath in the storm like a bullfrog snaring a dragonfly,
called out, 'Gimping soldiers, Commander, and dead guns?
Our war-craft longs, sunshine or sleet-storm, for action!
March into Trenton, steal the dawn and be master,
for winter's a god of bluster—your army's the real god!'
Washington hoped. He also knew where his life had
been for years: *I'm only a springtime planter,*
he guessed, *trying to nurse an acre of tenderfoot fir-trees.*
Roused, drained, baffled but clear-eyed, he saw that
only December appeared full of decision,
thundering now northwest, its lightning a fool's gold.
Pain came back from a song in the tavern, where David's
voice and harp had burned like tigering hearth-fire.
Vaguely he heard from John upbraiding the river,
'Why don't you freeze solid? Then we could all go
sliding giddy as Boston girls on the cold Charles.'

Since the storm had the last laugh at him, insult
south-wind adding to north-wind and belches of east-wind,
squalls crude as the drunken applause of a barroom,
all that Washington knew of almanacs, weather
soughed in his brain like Gates: a chorus of *Don't cross!*
But winter months by the Susquehanna River
hardly cheered him. He dreaded spring without money,
Congress enraged, the Trenton bubble a pricked plan.
Still he thought *I must cancel attack plans.*

Noise came first, shouts upriver. 'Another
John Sullivan?' Washington mused. 'Or another
brawl,' said Sullivan, 'caused by hours of delaying.'
'Take a few of my men, John,' Washington told him—
then a shot from that quarter startled him. 'Come, John,'

Washington said, 'and William, my man.' He picked out
Other mounted guards and instantly galloped
toward the musket-fire, hooves mud-kicking, dodging
campsites and briary gulches. *Crack!* And the second
shot amazed him more. He called to his man for a warning,
soon as William Lee cocked, Washington nodded.
Gunfire transformed plenty of sleet into steam-puffs.
Thousands promptly replaced them, dousing their horses.
Slowed to a canter, wary, the General came close.
One man down and gasping. Another lying
face in the mud. To others gathering round them
Washington asked loudly, 'Who's in command here?'
'Sergeant Claiborne Dunn, sir. I've sent for my Colonel,
Mordecai Gist.' Holding a downward pointing
musket the sergeant said, 'I heard from a ways off.
Two of them mad as roosters. After the first man
stabbed this man who's holding his belly, I ordered
Private Waterman here—sharpshooter, good man—
"Aim at the tree nearby." I called to them, "Stand still!"
They ignored me. I took the musket myself then,
aimed low but hit the ribcage. He's dead, sir.'

Washington knew the sergeant. Hessians had crazed him
bayoneting friends at the Battle of Brooklyn.
Dunn was raised in a Baltimore family of blunt men,
hammer-wielding steer slaughterers. Well-armed
now he carried a tomahawk, hanger and spontoon.
'Why the stabbing,' Washington asked as he walked up
close to the bodies. Dunn said, 'Commander, I don't know.'
Loss of blood already had neutered the two men's
movements and sounds. A doctor kneeling beside them
probed stab-wounds gently and gave up. 'He'll die soon.'
'Search them,' Washington said, as a colonel,
Mordecai Gist, reined in, followed by two aides.

Last year's captain of soldiers called Independents,
this year's major in Maryland regiments led by
Colonel William Smallwood, gentleman fighters
who had bravely, hopelessly, stalled the British
onslaught late last August, fallen to grapeshot,
drowned in Gowanus Creek in the Battle of Brooklyn—
Smallwood gashed, mending slowly, in bed still—
Gist was now the third Maryland's colonel.
Smartly saluting, he spoke out, 'General, Sergeant
Dunn's well known to me. The others'—he knelt down
close to the wounded man and the dead one—'are strangers.'

Dunn was finding papers. Washington made out
wet-ink horses, field-pieces, numbers of armed men.
Next was a map, scrawls like winds from opposing
quarters north and south: the Trenton attack plan.
Angle spies at work? Gangrene in my own ranks?
'Bring me a torch,' he said. 'These men could be traitors.'
Shortly the dead man's face was closer: Goliath's.
Close to the arm, a knife with already half-ice
puce on the blade. The General knew him—or never
truly had known him. He kept each spy at a distance,
kept each close and private. He'd given Goliath
sundry names, lifetimes, yes and the gold coins
Dunn now handed him. Paper from Congress
always had made Goliath laugh and demand gold.
But he'd turned, he'd turned. The Commander had ordered,
'Tell the British at Pennington Washington calls you
winter meat for the fox. He'll eat you in two days.'
Lung now burst by a musket bullet, Goliath's
blood made slush redden, barter for nothing.
More young soldiers gathered, looking like children
staring at back-yard loss, a tom with his blank face,
stela-stiff. Feeling the agony's not theirs,

23

still they remain close, they look for an elder's
word and gesture: how can psalms or gardenias
change the act, say good-bye or appease death?

Washington wondered who was the traitor's partner.
What's that glint on the ground nearby? A jew's harp?
Yes. Williams, the Camp David. The General
saw wounds in the belly, life-blood losing
slowly. He touched the harper's hand and asked him,
'Why did Goliath hurt you?' Trying to answer,
David's voice failed him. Shortly he whispered,
'Told me. General. Warn the Hessians. A dawn fight.'
Then he clutched his middle as though he had just lost
unborn life, a child torn from his entrails.

Washington tried feeding words to this poor tongue.
'So you told him not to. You fought him?' 'I asked him,'
David said, 'how betray them? He told me.
Army's hateful. General. Only the gold's good.'
Crying fraily as though a voice from the next world,
'Oh my Goliath! Little giant'—he coughed twice—
'killed our closeness.' Breathing slower, he whispered,
'Told me. General. No one's faithful on. Either
side, to king or. God. Americans murder. . .
both in the field. You too ruin. Your own men.
Force-marching. Fools at night in. A sleet-storm.'

Drained and dun in the random glance of the torchlight,
still the young man's face looked beautiful, light green
eyes and off-pink lips, hair in its gold hanks.
Washington asked, 'Why did he stab you?' 'Told me
join him,' David rasped. 'Sing my loathsome
songs. To Hessians. Make everyone. Hate war.'
Peace the Commander recalled in both Narragansett

24

teepee and Roger Williams' home. He remembered
David's line, 'War is folly on both sides.'
David answered, 'Could not join him. Commander.
Not when I saw you. Touched by Joseph. Warren's
death'—he winced abruptly. The General called out,
'Whiskey or rum for this man's pain.' 'You forget, sir,
someone said from the dark, 'the stomach's been opened.'

David found his harp, fingered the one wet
string and sighed. 'Dear Goliath. Punched me
when I cried, "Please. Don't leave me." He laughed and.
told me, "Quiet." General.' Pupils dilating,
suddenly David stared: 'A vision. I saw him
writhing pinned. Worm on a pavement. Dying
not in. my arms but close. Beside me. And far off.'

Washington had to lean closer, he must hear:
'When I yelled he. Damned and struck me. I felt white
cold lightning. My belly. A musket-ball then. Came
close. He stabbed me again. I heard a thud. In
his own chest. Hoofbeats. Goliath dragging us. Both down.'

Ears and Tongue bleeding, dying together.
Washington clasped the wrist, limp as the whole boy.
When he looked around, ghostlier downpour
stared back at him, ghostlier soldiers and north-wind.

Then he tingled. What he thought was a lifeless
Finger tapped his thumb. Ear at the boy's mouth,
'NIH-quah-SOOT-tam,' he heard. 'General, I change my
house. Longed for peace. At the wrong time.'
Gargled breath. 'Please, sir. Help the wounded.
Otherwise how. Is Washington better. Than *that* George?'

David tensed and a gust scattered the sudden
smell of shit. He retched weakly. 'My Jew's harp.'
One of his hands reached out, trembled and fell short.

Promptly a doctor crouched and felt. 'There is no pulse.'
Washington nodded, stood up slow as the oldest
pine in Virginia might, adding inches in ten years.
Duty poked him. Moments passed and he damned them.
Then he commanded, 'Bury them shortly. A parson?'
Someone raised a hand: 'I'll pray for them.' 'That one
surely betrayed us, General, no one should bless him,'
Dunn complained of Goliath. 'Let them be prayed for,'
Washington answered, mounting. But *You should not ride
yet* he thought, not sure why he should linger.

Much he'd listened to gladly over the past eight
months came back to him, hope no more than a single
half-red charcoal close to death in its own ash.
Samuel Adams, brewing beer and the best new
Cause in New England, told him *Remember the one word,
fairness*. He'd heard out Susan Danforth on Harlem
evenings last autumn: *This war is for women's
freedom too*. Now as he noticed sleet-blurred
men approaching in greater numbers—the sorry
brows of straw, driftwood elbows and raw knees—
cold and heat both seized him. For David,
foiling Goliath's plot, may have saved the morning.
Wild dreams of a sleet-mad victory teased him.
Anger at George the Third, at the sky, at Goliath's
gold-stained mind, all warmed the General's prowess.
Though an ebony gust and the army's revolting
march this blue-black night still tried to deter him.

David's song, if not his pulse: could it rouse each
lover and healer again recalled in McKonkey's?
Then as a man prayed for Goliath and David,
while the Cause and Samuel Adams could still breathe,
care built up in Washington's heart for this gimping
corps of farmer sons and Maryland teachers,
ashen boys of Jersey blacksmiths and marksmen
hailing from far-off western-spreading Virginia.
Exaltation fired him; grief and the sleet-storm
froze each impulse. The man sweated and shuddered.

Never a highly praised speech-maker, he called out,
'Look—at this traitor! A man dies if he sells out
trust like yours. This young harper and lover
died to make us *care*. Nothing proclaims it
louder than blood: your Cause is a great song!'

Officers murmured. The sergeant clapped but a motley
throng stared blankly. Washington reddened,
briskly dismounted, faced soldiers and bellowed,
'Now is your time! Each step and breath will be counted.
Cross that river! Move on the enemy right now!'

'Cross the river,' Sullivan seconded, 'right now!'
'Washington!' Colonel Gist hollered, and Dunn said,
'Follow the General!' William Lee, with a louder
voice and a pistol raised, yelled at them, 'Right now!'
Up and down the riverbank echoed them, 'Right now!'

Washington nodded, grimaced. 'It's started,'
he told Sullivan. *'Victory or Death* is the password,
John.' 'Can't get victory unless we go there,'
John said. 'And I am hardly ready to die yet,'

Washington said. 'I'll have to deal with a year's end,
this now dead day, it looks like a city
in ash. Jerusalem rubble? A burned Troy?'

Starting to mount, Washington spotted
the half-sunk harp of David, a memory of plain song.
Waving off Lee, he raised it himself. He saw its
lone string was broken, loosely dangling
like a dud, a diminished firecracker, trailing
grey, not red. *Reworked* he thought *could it still sing?*

About the Author

Born and raised in Rhode Island, he spent four years in the Navy before studying at Brown University for his Ph.D. in 1970. He enjoyed a teaching and writing career at Providence College while advancing to the rank of full Professor and traveling to many cities at home and abroad to deliver readings of his poetry and prose. He became the father of four daughters in his first marriage and now lives with his second wife, Dr. Beatrice Beebe, in New York City and in Newport, RI.

His most recent writing, in both fiction and narrative poetry, focuses on the struggle between opposed politicians, contrary lovers, and rival social systems. Put number one first, he often urges family and friends because you can't help others unless your own body and brain are up to it. So he often begins an exchange by asking, "How well have you been exercising lately, and are you sleeping and eating well, and"—his own first concern— "are you keeping up your *creative* life somehow?"

Also by Edward McCrorie

After a Cremation, poems (Thorp Springs Press, Berkeley, CA, 1974)

The Aeneid of Virgil, verse translation, Collector's Edition (Donald Grant Press, Providence, RI, 1991), library and trade editions (University of Michigan Press, Ann Arbor, MI, 1995)

Needle Man, poems (Chestnut Hills Press, Towson, MD, 1999)

The Odyssey of Homer, verse translation (The Johns Hopkins University Press), library and trade editions (Baltimore, MD, 2004 and 2006)

Gone Games, poems (Brick House Books, Baltimore, MD 2010)

The Iliad of Homer, verse translation, library and trade editions (The Johns Hopkins University Press, Baltimore, MD, 2012)

Pretend Ballads, poems inspired by the children of September 11, 2001 (International Psychoanalytic Books, 25-79 31st Street, Astoria, New York, 11102)

www.ingramcontent.com/pod-product-compliance
Lightning Source LLC
Chambersburg PA
CBHW071753090426
42738CB00011B/2671